Table of Contents

Toffee Crunch Muffins

$1^1/_2$ cups all-purpose flour
$^1/_3$ cup packed brown sugar
2 teaspoons baking powder
$^1/_2$ teaspoon baking soda
$^1/_2$ teaspoon salt
$^1/_2$ cup milk
$^1/_2$ cup sour cream
3 tablespoons butter, melted
1 egg, beaten
1 teaspoon vanilla
3 bars (1.4 ounces each) chocolate-covered toffee, chopped and divided

1. Preheat oven to 400°F. Grease 36 mini ($1^3/_4$-inch) muffin cups; set aside.

2. Combine flour, brown sugar, baking powder, baking soda and salt in large bowl. Combine milk, sour cream, butter, egg and vanilla in small bowl until well blended. Stir into flour mixture just until moistened. Fold in two-thirds of toffee. Spoon into prepared muffin cups, filling almost full. Sprinkle remaining toffee evenly over tops of muffins.

3. Bake 16 to 18 minutes or until toothpick inserted into centers comes out clean. Remove from pans. Cool on wire racks 10 minutes.

Makes 36 mini muffins

Boston Brown Bread

$^1/_2$ cup rye flour
$^1/_2$ cup yellow cornmeal
$^1/_2$ cup whole wheat flour
3 tablespoons sugar
1 teaspoon baking soda
$^3/_4$ teaspoon salt
$^1/_2$ cup chopped walnuts
$^1/_2$ cup raisins
1 cup buttermilk
$^1/_3$ cup molasses
Boiling water

1. Grease well 3 (16-ounce) vegetable cans and 1 side of 3 (6-inch) square foil pieces with shortening; set aside.

2. Combine rye flour, cornmeal, whole wheat flour, sugar, baking soda and salt in large bowl. Stir in walnuts and raisins. Combine buttermilk and molasses in medium bowl with wire whisk until smooth. Add buttermilk mixture to dry ingredients; stir until well mixed.

3. Spoon mixture evenly into prepared cans. Place 1 piece of foil, greased side down, on top of each can. Secure foil with rubber bands or cotton string. Place filled cans in deep 4-quart saucepan or Dutch oven. Pour boiling water around cans so water comes halfway up sides of cans. (Make sure foil tops do not touch boiling water.)

4. Bring to a boil over high heat. Reduce heat to low. Cover; simmer (water should be bubbling very slowly) $1^1/_4$ to $1^1/_2$ hours or until wooden skewer inserted into center of bread comes out clean. Remove cans from saucepan. Immediately run knife around inside edges of cans to loosen breads. Invert and gently shake breads out of cans. Cool completely on wire rack.

Makes 3 loaves

Rosemary Breadsticks

$^2/_3$ cup reduced-fat (2%) milk
$^1/_4$ cup finely chopped fresh chives
2 teaspoons baking powder
1 teaspoon finely chopped fresh rosemary *or* $^1/_2$ teaspoon dried rosemary, crushed
$^3/_4$ teaspoon salt
$^1/_2$ teaspoon freshly ground black pepper
$^3/_4$ cup whole wheat flour
$^3/_4$ cup all-purpose flour
Nonstick cooking spray

1. Combine milk, chives, baking powder, rosemary, salt and pepper in large bowl; mix well. Stir in flours, $^1/_2$ cup at a time, until blended. Turn onto floured surface and knead dough about 5 minutes or until smooth and elastic, adding more flour if dough is sticky. Cover; let stand 30 minutes at room temperature.

2. Preheat oven to 375°F. Spray baking sheet with cooking spray. Divide dough into 12 balls, about $1^1/_4$ ounces each. Roll each ball into long thin rope; place on prepared baking sheet. Lightly spray breadsticks with cooking spray. Bake about 12 minutes or until bottoms are golden brown. Turn breadsticks over; bake about 10 minutes more or until golden brown.

Makes 12 breadsticks

Peanut Butter Bread

$^3/_4$ cup packed brown sugar
$^1/_2$ cup peanut butter
3 tablespoons butter, cut into 3 pieces
2 eggs
1 cup all-purpose flour
$^1/_2$ cup whole wheat flour
2 teaspoons baking powder
$^1/_2$ teaspoon ground cinnamon
$^1/_4$ teaspoon salt
$^1/_4$ teaspoon ground nutmeg
$^1/_4$ teaspoon ground allspice
$^2/_3$ cup milk
$^1/_2$ teaspoon vanilla
1 cup chopped peanuts

1. Preheat oven to 325°F. Grease $8^1/_2 \times 4^1/_2 \times 2^1/_2$-inch loaf pan. Fit processor with steel blade. Measure brown sugar, peanut butter and butter into work bowl. Process until smooth, about 10 seconds. Add eggs one at a time through feed tube with processor on. With processor off, add flours, baking powder, cinnamon, salt, nutmeg and allspice. Process with on/off pulses until mixed.

2. Pour milk and vanilla into mixture. Process just until moistened. Do not overprocess. Batter should be lumpy. Sprinkle peanuts over batter. Process just until peanuts are mixed into batter.

3. Pour batter into prepared loaf pan. Bake until toothpick inserted into center comes out clean, about 1 hour. Cool bread 15 minutes in pan. Remove from pan and cool on wire rack.

Makes 1 loaf

Double Chocolate Zucchini Muffins

2$\frac{1}{3}$ cups all-purpose flour

1$\frac{1}{4}$ cups sugar

$\frac{1}{3}$ cup unsweetened cocoa powder

2 teaspoons baking powder

1$\frac{1}{2}$ teaspoons ground cinnamon

1 teaspoon baking soda

$\frac{1}{2}$ teaspoon salt

1 cup sour cream

$\frac{1}{2}$ cup vegetable oil

2 eggs, beaten

$\frac{1}{4}$ cup milk

1 cup milk chocolate chips

1 cup shredded zucchini

1. Preheat oven to 400°F. Grease 12 jumbo (3$\frac{1}{2}$-inch) muffin cups.

2. Combine flour, sugar, cocoa, baking powder, cinnamon, baking soda and salt in large bowl. Combine sour cream, oil, eggs and milk in small bowl until blended; stir into flour mixture just until moistened. Fold in chips and zucchini. Spoon into prepared muffin cups, filling $\frac{1}{2}$ full.

3. Bake 25 to 30 minutes until wooden toothpick inserted into centers comes out clean. Cool in pan on wire rack 5 minutes. Remove from pan. Cool on wire rack. Store tightly covered at room temperature.

Makes 12 jumbo muffins

Golden Eggnog Holiday Braid

2 tablespoons warm water (110°F)
2 tablespoons sugar
1 package ($^1/_4$ ounce) active dry yeast
$2^1/_2$ cups all-purpose flour
2 tablespoons butter, cut into 2 pieces
1 teaspoon salt
$^1/_4$ teaspoon ground nutmeg
$^1/_2$ to $^3/_4$ cup dairy eggnog, at room temperature
    Vegetable oil
    Dairy eggnog
    Sliced almonds

1. Combine warm water, sugar and yeast in small bowl. Let stand about 5 minutes or until bubbly.

2. Fit processor with steel blade. Measure flour, butter, salt and nutmeg into work bowl. Process until mixed. Add yeast mixture; process until blended.

3. Turn on processor and slowly drizzle just enough eggnog through feed tube so dough forms a ball that cleans sides of bowl. Process until ball turns around bowl 25 times. Let dough stand in bowl 1 to 2 minutes.

4. Turn on processor and drizzle in enough remaining eggnog to make dough smooth and no longer sticky. Process until dough turns around bowl 15 times.

5. Let dough stand in bowl 10 minutes. Turn dough onto lightly floured surface and shape into ball. Place in greased bowl, turning to grease all sides. Cover; let stand in warm place (85°F) 1 hour or until doubled in bulk.

6. Punch down dough. Let stand 10 minutes. Divide into 3 equal parts. Shape each part into strand 20 inches long. Braid strands together; tuck ends under and pinch to seal. Place on greased cookie sheet. Brush with oil and let stand in warm place until doubled, about 45 minutes.

7. Preheat oven to 375°F. Brush braid with eggnog and sprinkle with almonds. Bake until golden, 25 to 30 minutes. Remove braid from cookie sheet. Cool on wire rack.

Makes 1 loaf

Apple Butter Spice Muffins

$^1/_2$ cup sugar

1 teaspoon ground cinnamon

$^1/_4$ teaspoon ground nutmeg

$^1/_8$ teaspoon ground allspice

$^1/_2$ cup pecans or walnuts, chopped

2 cups all-purpose flour

2 teaspoons baking powder

$^1/_4$ teaspoon salt

1 cup milk

$^1/_4$ cup vegetable oil

1 egg

$^1/_4$ cup apple butter

1. Preheat oven to 400°F. Grease 12 standard ($2^1/_2$-inch) muffin cups or line with paper baking cups.

2. Combine sugar, cinnamon, nutmeg and allspice in large bowl. Toss 2 tablespoons sugar mixture with pecans in small bowl; set aside. Add flour, baking powder and salt to remaining sugar mixture.

3. Combine milk, oil and egg in medium bowl. Stir into flour mixture just until moistened.

4. Spoon 1 tablespoon batter into each prepared muffin cup. Spoon 1 teaspoon apple butter into each cup. Spoon remaining batter evenly over apple butter. Sprinkle reserved pecan mixture over each muffin. Bake 20 to 25 minutes or until golden brown and toothpick inserted into centers comes out clean. Immediately remove from pan; cool on wire rack 10 minutes.

Makes 12 muffins

Cinnamon-Raisin Bread

$^{1}/_{2}$ cup plus 1 teaspoon sugar, divided
$^{1}/_{4}$ cup warm water (110°F)
1 package ($^{1}/_{4}$ ounce) active dry yeast
3 to 3$^{1}/_{2}$ cups all-purpose flour, divided
1 teaspoon salt
$^{2}/_{3}$ cup warm milk (105° to 115°F)
3 tablespoons butter, softened
1 whole egg
1 egg, separated
1 teaspoon vanilla
$^{3}/_{4}$ cup raisins
1 tablespoon ground cinnamon
1 tablespoon butter, melted
1 tablespoon water

1. Combine 1 teaspoon sugar, warm water and yeast in small bowl. Let stand 5 minutes or until bubbly.

2. Combine 1$^{1}/_{2}$ cups flour, $^{1}/_{4}$ cup sugar and salt in large bowl. Gradually beat yeast mixture, warm milk and softened butter into flour mixture with electric mixer until combined.

3. Beat in whole egg, egg yolk and vanilla on low speed. Increase speed to medium; beat 2 minutes. Add enough additional flour to make soft dough.

4. Turn out onto lightly floured surface. Knead 5 minutes adding enough remaining flour to make a smooth and elastic dough. Knead in raisins; shape dough into ball. Place dough in large greased bowl; turn once to grease surface. Cover and let rise in warm place 1 hour or until doubled in bulk.

5. Punch down dough; knead on lightly floured surface 1 minute. Cover; let rest 10 minutes. Grease 9×5-inch loaf pan; set aside. Combine remaining $^{1}/_{4}$ cup sugar and cinnamon. Reserve 1 tablespoon mixture.

6. Roll dough into 20×9-inch rectangle with floured rolling pin. Brush with butter. Sprinkle cinnamon mixture over butter. Roll dough from long side into log. Pinch ends and seam to seal. Place loaf, seam side down, in prepared pan. Cover; let rise in warm place 1 hour or until doubled in bulk.

7. Preheat oven to 350°F. Combine egg white and water in small bowl. Brush loaf with egg white mixture; sprinkle with reserved cinnamon mixture.

8. Bake 40 to 45 minutes or until loaf sounds hollow when tapped. Immediately remove from pan; cool completely on wire rack.

Makes 1 loaf

Brunchtime Sour Cream Cupcakes

1 cup (2 sticks) butter, softened
2 cups plus 4 teaspoons sugar, divided
2 eggs
1 cup sour cream
1 teaspoon almond extract
2 cups all-purpose flour
1 teaspoon salt
$^1/_2$ teaspoon baking soda
1 cup chopped walnuts
1$^1/_2$ teaspoons ground cinnamon
$^1/_8$ teaspoon ground nutmeg

1. Preheat oven to 350°F. Grease 18 standard (2$^1/_2$-inch) muffin cups or line with paper baking cups.

2. Beat butter and 2 cups sugar in large bowl. Add eggs, one at a time, beating well after each addition. Blend in sour cream and almond extract. Combine flour, salt and baking soda in medium bowl. Add to butter mixture; mix well.

3. Stir together remaining 4 teaspoons sugar, walnuts, cinnamon and nutmeg in small bowl.

4. Fill prepared muffin cups $^1/_3$ full with batter; sprinkle evenly with $^2/_3$ of the walnut mixture. Cover with remaining batter. Sprinkle with remaining walnut mixture.

5. Bake 25 to 30 minutes or until toothpick inserted into centers comes out clean. Remove cupcakes from pan; cool on wire rack.

Makes 1$^1/_2$ dozen cupcakes

Tomato-Artichoke Focaccia

    1 package (16 ounces) hot roll mix
    2 tablespoons wheat bran
1¼ cups hot water
    4 teaspoons olive oil, divided
    1 cup thinly sliced onions
    2 cloves garlic, minced
    4 ounces oil-packed sun-dried tomatoes, drained and cut into strips
    1 cup canned artichoke hearts, cut into quarters
    1 tablespoon minced fresh rosemary
    2 tablespoons shredded Parmesan cheese

1. Preheat oven to 400°F. Combine dry ingredients and yeast packet from hot roll mix in large bowl. Add bran; mix well. Stir in hot water and 2 teaspoons oil. Knead dough about 5 minutes or until ingredients are blended.

2. Spray 2 (9-inch) round cake pans with nonstick cooking spray. Press dough onto bottom of prepared pans. Cover; let rise 15 minutes.

3. Heat 1 teaspoon oil in medium skillet over low heat. Add onions and garlic; cook and stir 2 to 3 minutes until onions are tender.

4. Brush surface of dough with remaining 1 teaspoon oil. Top dough with onion mixture, tomatoes, artichokes and rosemary. Sprinkle with Parmesan.

5. Bake 25 to 30 minutes or until lightly browned on top.

Makes 16 servings

Walnut–Chocolate Quick Bread

1½ cups milk
1 cup sugar
⅓ cup vegetable oil
1 egg, beaten
1 tablespoon molasses
1 teaspoon vanilla
3 cups all-purpose flour
3 tablespoons unsweetened cocoa powder
2 teaspoons baking soda
2 teaspoons baking powder
1 teaspoon salt
1 cup chocolate chips
½ cup walnuts, coarsely chopped

1. Preheat oven to 350°F. Grease four mini (5×3-inch) loaf pans; set aside.

2. Combine milk, sugar, oil, egg, molasses and vanilla in medium bowl. Stir until sugar is dissolved.

3. Combine flour, cocoa, baking soda, baking powder and salt in large bowl. Add chocolate chips, walnuts and milk mixture; stir just until combined. Pour into prepared pans.

4. Bake 30 minutes or until toothpick inserted into centers of loaves comes out clean. Cool in pans 15 minutes. Remove from pans and cool on wire racks. *Makes 4 small loaves*

Muffin Variation: Preheat oven to 375°F. Spoon batter into 12 greased muffin cups. Bake 20 minutes or until toothpicks inserted into centers come out clean. Makes 12 muffins.

Dresden Stollen

$^1/_4$ cup *each* golden raisins, chopped candied cherries, slivered almonds, and
    candied orange peel
2 tablespoons brandy or rum
$^1/_4$ cup warm water (110°F)
4 tablespoons sugar, divided
2 packages ($^1/_4$ ounce each) active dry yeast
4 pieces lemon peel (each about $2 \times ^1/_2$-inch)
$2^3/_4$ cups all-purpose flour
$^1/_3$ cup cold butter, cut into 5 pieces
$^1/_2$ teaspoon salt
1 large egg
$^1/_2$ teaspoon almond extract
2 to 5 tablespoons milk
2 tablespoons butter, melted and divided
1 large egg white, lightly beaten
3 tablespoons powdered sugar

1. Mix raisins, cherries, almonds, orange peel and brandy in small bowl; reserve. Combine water, 1 tablespoon sugar and yeast in small bowl. Let stand about 5 minutes until bubbly.

2. Place remaining 3 tablespoons sugar and lemon peel in food processor. Process until peel is minced. Add flour, cold butter and salt. Process until mixed. Add yeast mixture, egg and almond extract; process until blended.

3. With processor on, slowly drizzle enough milk through feed tube so dough forms ball that cleans sides of bowl. Process until ball turns around bowl about 25 times. Let dough stand 1 to 2 minutes.

4. With processor on, drizzle in enough remaining milk to make smooth, satiny dough. Process until dough turns around bowl about 15 times.

5. Turn dough onto lightly floured surface. Shape into ball, cover and let stand 20 minutes.

6. Knead fruit mixture into dough on floured surface adding additional flour, if needed, to keep dough from sticking. Shape dough into ball and place in lightly greased bowl, turning to grease surface. Cover; let stand in warm place (85°F) about 1 hour or until doubled in bulk.

7. Punch down dough. Roll or pat dough into 9×7-inch oval on large greased

cookie sheet. Brush with 1 tablespoon butter. Make a crease in dough lengthwise with handle of wooden spoon, just off center. Fold smaller section over larger one. Brush top with egg white. Cover; let stand in warm place 45 minutes or until almost doubled in bulk.

9. Preheat oven to 350°F. Bake 25 to 30 minutes or until browned. Remove immediately from cookie sheet and place on wire rack. Brush with remaining 1 tablespoon butter. Sift powdered sugar over bread.   *Makes 1 loaf*

Cranberry Pecan Muffins

$1^3/_4$ cups all-purpose flour
$^1/_2$ cup packed light brown sugar
$2^1/_2$ teaspoons baking powder
$^1/_2$ teaspoon salt
$^3/_4$ cup milk
$^1/_4$ cup butter, melted
1 egg, beaten
1 cup chopped fresh cranberries
$^1/_3$ cup chopped pecans
1 teaspoon grated lemon peel

1. Preheat oven to 400°F. Grease 36 mini ($1^3/_4$-inch) muffin cups.

2. Combine flour, brown sugar, baking powder and salt in large bowl. Combine milk, butter and egg in small bowl until blended; stir into flour mixture just until moistened. Fold in cranberries, pecans and lemon peel. Spoon into prepared muffin cups, filling almost full.

3. Bake 15 to 17 minutes or until toothpick inserted into centers comes out clean. Remove from pans. Cool on wire racks. *Makes 36 mini muffins*

Pecan-Cinnamon Sticky Buns

3 to 3$\frac{1}{2}$ cups all-purpose flour
$\frac{1}{3}$ cup nonfat dry milk
1 package ($\frac{1}{4}$ ounce) rapid-rise active dry yeast
1 teaspoon salt
1 egg, beaten
5 tablespoons butter, melted, divided
1 cup water
$\frac{3}{4}$ cup plus 2 tablespoons honey, divided
$\frac{3}{4}$ cup chopped pecans
$\frac{1}{4}$ cup packed brown sugar
2 teaspoons ground cinnamon

1. Combine 3 cups flour, milk powder, yeast and salt in large bowl. Place water and 2 tablespoons honey in small saucepan; heat until very warm (120°F), stirring to dissolve honey. Pour into flour mixture; beat on low speed of electric mixer until combined. Beat in 3 tablespoons melted butter and egg until dough forms.

2. Knead dough on well-floured board 10 minutes, adding additional flour as necessary to make dough smooth and elastic. Shape into ball; place in large greased bowl. Turn to grease surface. Cover; let rise in warm place 30 to 40 minutes or until doubled in bulk.

3. Meanwhile, spread remaining $\frac{3}{4}$ cup honey evenly in bottom of 9-inch square baking pan; sprinkle with pecans; set aside.

4. Punch dough down; turn out onto floured surface. Pat or roll dough into 15×9-inch rectangle. Brush dough with remaining 2 tablespoons butter. Mix brown sugar and cinnamon in small bowl; sprinkle over butter. Roll dough from long side into log; pinch edges to seal. Cut into 12 slices about 1$\frac{1}{4}$ inches thick. Arrange in prepared pan; cover and let rise 25 minutes.

5. Preheat oven to 350°F. Bake buns 30 minutes until golden. Cool slightly; invert onto plate. *Makes 12 buns*

Apple Raisin Walnut Muffins

2 cups all-purpose flour
$^{3}/_{4}$ cup granulated sugar
2 teaspoons baking powder
1 teaspoon ground cinnamon
$^{1}/_{2}$ teaspoon baking soda
$^{1}/_{2}$ teaspoon salt
$^{1}/_{4}$ teaspoon ground nutmeg
$^{3}/_{4}$ cup plus 2 tablespoons milk
$^{1}/_{3}$ cup butter, melted
2 eggs, beaten
1 cup chopped dried apples
$^{1}/_{2}$ cup golden raisins
$^{1}/_{2}$ cup chopped walnuts

1. Preheat oven to 350°F. Grease 6 jumbo ($3^{1}/_{2}$-inch) muffin cups. Combine flour, sugar, baking powder, baking soda, cinnamon, salt and nutmeg in large bowl.

2. Beat together milk, eggs and butter in small bowl. Stir into flour mixture just until blended. Gently fold in apples, raisins and walnuts. Fill prepared muffin cups $^{3}/_{4}$ full.

3. Bake 25 to 30 minutes or until toothpick inserted into centers comes out clean. Cool in pan 2 minutes; remove muffins to wire rack. Serve warm or at room temperature.

Makes 6 jumbo muffins

Lemony Banana–Walnut Bread

$^2/_3$ cup shortening

1 cup granulated sugar

2 eggs

$1^1/_2$ cups mashed ripe bananas (about 3 medium)

7 tablespoons fresh lemon juice (about 3 lemons), divided

2 cups all-purpose flour

1 teaspoon baking soda

1 teaspoon baking powder

$^1/_2$ teaspoon salt

$^1/_2$ cup chopped walnuts

1 tablespoon grated lemon peel

$^1/_2$ cup powdered sugar

1. Preheat oven to 325°F. Grease 2 ($8^1/_2 \times 4^1/_2$-inch) loaf pans.

2. Beat shortening and granulated sugar in large bowl with electric mixer at medium speed until well blended. Add eggs, 1 at a time, mixing well after each addition. Blend in bananas and 6 tablespoons juice. Combine flour, baking soda, baking powder and salt in medium bowl. Add to banana mixture; mix until blended. Stir in walnuts and lemon peel. Pour evenly into prepared pans.

3. Bake 50 to 60 minutes until wooden toothpick inserted into centers comes out clean. Remove from pans; cool completely on wire racks.

4. Combine powdered sugar and remaining 1 tablespoon juice in small bowl; stir until smooth. Drizzle over cooled loaves. *Makes 2 loaves*

Quick Pumpkin Bread

1 cup packed light brown sugar
$^1/_3$ cup cold butter, cut into 5 pieces
2 eggs
1 cup solid-pack pumpkin
$1^1/_2$ cups all-purpose flour
$^1/_2$ cup whole wheat flour
$1^1/_2$ teaspoons pumpkin pie spice
1 teaspoon baking soda
$^3/_4$ teaspoon salt
$^1/_2$ teaspoon baking powder
$^1/_4$ teaspoon ground cardamom (optional)
$^1/_2$ cup dark raisins or chopped, pitted dates
$^1/_2$ cup chopped pecans or walnuts

1. Preheat oven to 350°F. Fit processor with steel blade. Measure sugar and butter into work bowl. Process until smooth, about 10 seconds.

2. Turn on processor and add eggs one at a time through feed tube. Add pumpkin, flours, pie spice, baking soda, salt, baking powder and cardamom, if desired. Process just until flour is moistened, about 5 seconds. Batter should be lumpy.

3. Sprinkle raisins and nuts over batter. Process using on/off pulsing action 2 or 3 times or just until raisins and nuts are mixed into batter.

4. Turn batter into greased 9×5-inch loaf pan or 3 greased mini (5×3-inch) loaf pans. Bake until toothpick inserted in center comes out clean, about 1 hour for larger loaf or 30 to 35 minutes for smaller loaves. Cool bread 15 minutes in pan. Remove from pan and cool on wire rack.

Makes 1 large or 3 small loaves

Note: Whole wheat flour can be omitted, if desired, and a total of 2 cups all-purpose flour used instead.

Maple-Pumpkin-Pecan Twist

    1 can (15 ounces) solid-pack pumpkin
    1 cup water
$^1/_2$ cup shortening
    7 to 8 cups all-purpose flour, divided
    2 cups pecans, coarsely chopped
$^1/_2$ cup sugar
    2 packages ($^1/_4$ ounce each) active dry yeast
    2 teaspoons salt
    2 eggs
    2 teaspoons maple flavoring, divided
    6 to 8 tablespoons milk
    2 cups powdered sugar

1. Heat pumpkin, water and shortening in medium saucepan over medium heat until shortening is melted and temperature reaches 120° to 130°F.

2. Combine 4 cups flour, pecans, sugar, yeast and salt in large bowl. Add pumpkin mixture, eggs and 1 teaspoon maple flavoring; beat vigorously with electric mixer 2 minutes. Add remaining flour, $^1/_4$ cup at a time, until dough begins to pull away from side of bowl. Knead dough on lightly floured surface 10 minutes or until smooth and elastic, adding flour as needed to prevent sticking. Shape dough into ball. Place in large lightly greased bowl; turn once to grease surface. Cover; let rise in warm place about 1 hour or until doubled in bulk.

3. Turn dough out onto lightly floured surface; divide into four pieces. Shape each piece into 24-inch-long rope. Twist 2 ropes together; pinch ends. Shape into ring. Place on lightly greased baking sheet. Repeat with remaining 2 ropes. Cover; let rise in warm place 45 minutes.

4. Preheat oven to 375°F. Bake 25 minutes or until golden brown. Immediately remove from baking sheets; cool on wire rack 20 minutes.

5. Combine remaining 1 teaspoon maple flavoring and 6 tablespoons milk in small bowl. Whisk milk mixture and powdered sugar together in medium bowl. If icing is too thick, add remaining milk, 1 teaspoon at a time, until of desired consistency. Drizzle over loaves. *Makes 2 large twists*

Cranberry Raisin Nut Bread

1^1/$_2$ cups all-purpose flour
^{3}/$_4$ cup packed light brown sugar
1^1/$_2$ teaspoons baking powder
^{1}/$_2$ teaspoon baking soda
^{1}/$_2$ teaspoon ground cinnamon
^{1}/$_2$ teaspoon ground nutmeg
1 cup coarsely chopped fresh or frozen cranberries
^{1}/$_2$ cup golden raisins
^{1}/$_2$ cup coarsely chopped pecans
1 tablespoon grated orange peel
2 eggs
^{3}/$_4$ cup milk
3 tablespoons butter, melted
1 teaspoon vanilla
Cranberry-Orange Spread (recipe follows, optional)

1. Preheat oven to 350°F. Grease 8^1/$_2$×4^1/$_2$-inch loaf pan.

2. Combine flour, brown sugar, baking powder, baking soda, cinnamon and nutmeg in large bowl. Stir in cranberries, raisins, pecans and orange peel. Mix eggs, milk, butter and vanilla in small bowl until combined; stir into flour mixture just until moistened. Spoon into prepared pan.

3. Bake 55 to 60 minutes or until wooden toothpick inserted into center comes out clean. Cool in pan 15 minutes. Remove from pan and cool completely on wire rack. Store tightly wrapped in plastic wrap at room temperature. Serve with Cranberry-Orange Spread, if desired.

Makes 1 loaf

Cranberry-Orange Spread

1 package (8 ounces) cream cheese, softened
1 package (3 ounces) cream cheese, softened
1 container (12 ounces) cranberry-orange sauce
³/₄ cup chopped pecans

Combine cream cheese and cranberry-orange sauce in small bowl; stir until blended. Stir in pecans. Store in refrigerator.   *Makes about 3 cups spread*

Petit Pain au Chocolate

1 cup plus 1 tablespoon milk, divided
3 tablespoons butter, at room temperature
3 to 3½ cups all-purpose flour
3 tablespoons granulated sugar
1 package (¼ ounce) active dry yeast
1 teaspoon salt
1 egg, lightly beaten
1 milk chocolate candy bar (6 ounces), cut into 16 pieces
2 teaspoons colored sugar

1. Combine 1 cup milk and butter in small saucepan. Heat over low heat until mixture is 120° to 130°F. (Butter does not need to completely melt.)

2. Combine 3 cups flour, granulated sugar, yeast and salt in large bowl. Gradually stir milk mixture and egg into flour mixture to make soft dough.

3. Turn dough out onto lightly floured surface. Knead about 10 minutes, adding enough remaining flour to make smooth and elastic dough. Shape into ball. Place in large greased bowl; turn once to grease surface. Cover; let rise in warm place about 1 hour or until doubled in bulk.

4. Punch down dough. Knead dough on lightly floured surface 1 minute. Roll dough into log; cut into 8 pieces. Roll each piece into 6-inch round. Place 2 pieces chocolate in center of each round and fold edges up around chocolate. Pinch to seal seams.

5. Place rolls seam side down 3 inches apart on lightly greased baking sheet. Cover rolls with towel and let rise in warm place 20 to 30 minutes or until slightly puffed. Brush tops with remaining 1 tablespoon milk. Sprinkle with colored sugar.

6. Preheat oven to 400°F. Bake 12 to 15 minutes or until rolls are golden brown.

Makes 8 rolls

Tex-Mex Quick Bread

1 1/2 cups all-purpose flour
 1 cup (4 ounces) shredded Monterey Jack cheese
 1/2 cup cornmeal
 1/2 cup sun-dried tomatoes, coarsely chopped
 1 can (about 4 ounces) black olives, drained and chopped
 1/4 cup sugar
1 1/2 teaspoons baking powder
 1 teaspoon baking soda
 1 cup milk
 1 can (about 4 ounces) green chilies, drained and chopped
 1/4 cup olive oil
 1 egg, beaten

1. Preheat oven to 325°F. Grease 9×5-inch loaf pan or 4 mini (5×3-inch) loaf pans; set aside.

2. Combine flour, cheese, cornmeal, tomatoes, olives, sugar, baking powder and baking soda in large bowl.

3. Combine remaining ingredients in small bowl. Add to flour mixture; stir just until combined. Pour into prepared pan. Bake 9×5-inch loaf 45 minutes and 5×3-inch loaves 30 minutes or until toothpick inserted near center of loaf comes out clean. Cool in pan 15 minutes. Remove from pan and cool on wire rack.

Blueberry Cheesecake Muffins

1 package (8 ounces) cream cheese, softened
1 cup plus 1 tablespoon no-calorie sugar substitute for baking, divided
2 eggs
1 teaspoon grated lemon peel
1 teaspoon vanilla
$^3/_4$ cup bran flakes cereal
$^1/_2$ cup all-purpose flour
$^1/_2$ cup soy flour
2 teaspoons baking powder
$^1/_4$ teaspoon salt
$^3/_4$ cup milk
3 tablespoons melted butter
4 tablespoons no-sugar-added blueberry fruit spread
$^1/_2$ teaspoon ground cinnamon

1. Preheat oven to 350°F. Spray 12 muffin cups with nonstick cooking spray.

2. Beat cream cheese in medium bowl at high speed of electric mixer until smooth. Beat in $^3/_4$ cup sugar substitute, 1 egg, lemon peel and vanilla.

3. Stir together cereal, flours, $^1/_4$ cup sugar substitute, baking powder and salt in medium bowl. In small bowl, whisk milk, butter and remaining egg until blended; pour over cereal mixture. Mix gently just until blended.

4. Spoon about 2 tablespoons batter into each muffin cup. Spread 1 teaspoon fruit spread over batter. Spread cream cheese mixture over fruit spread. Combine remaining 1 tablespoon sugar substitute and cinnamon; sprinkle mixture evenly over cream cheese mixture.

5. Bake 30 to 35 minutes or until toothpicks inserted into centers come out clean. Cool muffins 10 minutes in pan on wire rack. Remove muffins from pan and cool. Serve warm or at room temperature. Refrigerate leftover muffins. *Makes 12 muffins*

Mediterranean Bread Braid

2 teaspoons dried basil
1 teaspoon dried oregano
$^1/_2$ teaspoon dried rosemary
$^1/_4$ teaspoon garlic powder
1 package (11 ounces) refrigerated French bread dough
2 ounces olives, pitted and finely chopped (about 16)
2 teaspoons olive oil

1. Preheat oven to 350°F.

2. Combine basil, oregano, rosemary and garlic powder in small bowl.

3. Lightly spray baking sheet with nonstick cooking spray. Place dough roll on baking sheet; unroll. Sprinkle evenly with olives and basil mixture. Cut lengthwise into 3 strips. Fold each strip in half lengthwise, creating 3 rope-like strips. Braid bread and tuck ends under slightly.

4. Bake 25 minutes or until bread is golden and sounds hollow when lightly tapped.

5. Remove from oven; place on cutting board to cool. Brush olive oil over top.

Makes 12 servings (1 loaf)

Tip: Peak flavors are reached by allowing the bread to cool to room temperature.

Date Nut Bread

1½ cups water
1½ cups coarsely chopped, pitted dates
½ cup packed light brown sugar
2 tablespoons butter, at room temperature
1 egg
2½ cups all-purpose flour
1 cup chopped pecans or walnuts
1 teaspoon baking soda
½ teaspoon salt

1. Bring water to a boil in small saucepan. Stir in dates. Remove from heat and cool until lukewarm (about 110°F). Reserve. Preheat oven to 350°F. Grease 9×5×3-inch loaf pan.

2. Fit processor with steel blade. Measure brown sugar and butter into work bowl. Process on/off 3 or 4 times to mix. Add egg; process until smooth, about 10 seconds. Add date mixture to sugar mixture. Process on/off 4 or 5 times.

3. Add flour, nuts, baking soda and salt to date mixture. Process on/off 8 to 10 times, or just until flour is moistened. Do not overprocess. Batter should be lumpy.

4. Pour batter into prepared loaf pan. Bake until toothpick inserted into center comes out clean, about 1¼ hours. (If bread browns too quickly, cover loosely with aluminum foil during last 15 to 20 minutes of baking.) Cool bread 15 minutes in pan. Remove from pan and cool on wire rack.

Makes 1 loaf

A gift from the kitchen of _____

For: _____

A gift from the kitchen of _____

For: _____

A gift from the kitchen of _____

For: _____

*A gift from the kitchen of*_____

For: _____

*A gift from the kitchen of*_____

For: _____

*A gift from the kitchen of*_____

For: _____

A gift from the kitchen of _____

For: _____

A gift from the kitchen of _____

For: _____

A gift from the kitchen of _____

For: _____

A gift from the kitchen of _____

For: _____

A gift from the kitchen of _____

For: _____

A gift from the kitchen of _____

For: _____

A gift from the kitchen of_____

For: _____

A gift from the kitchen of_____

For: _____

A gift from the kitchen of_____

For: _____

A gift from the kitchen of_____

For: _____

A gift from the kitchen of_____

For: _____

A gift from the kitchen of_____

For: _____

A gift from the kitchen of _____

For: _____

A gift from the kitchen of _____

For: _____

A gift from the kitchen of _____

For: _____

A gift from the kitchen of_____

For: _____

A gift from the kitchen of_____

For: _____

A gift from the kitchen of_____

For: _____

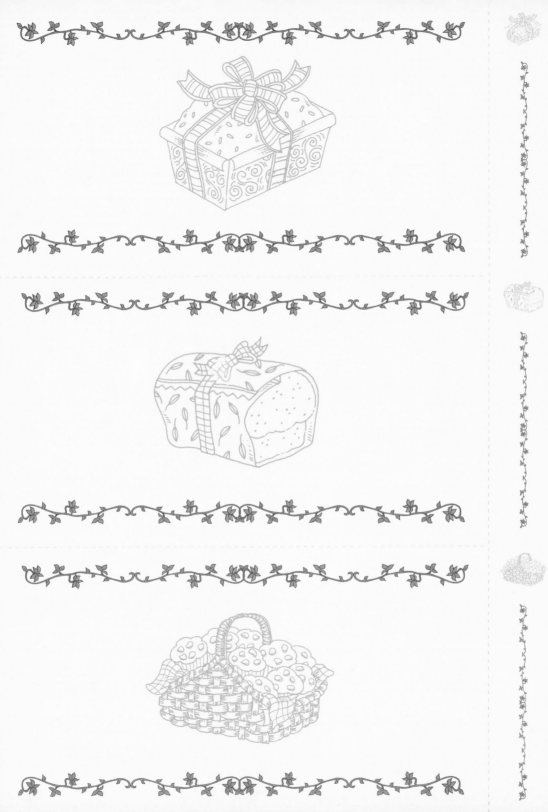

A gift from the kitchen of _____

For: _____

A gift from the kitchen of _____

For: _____

A gift from the kitchen of _____

For: _____

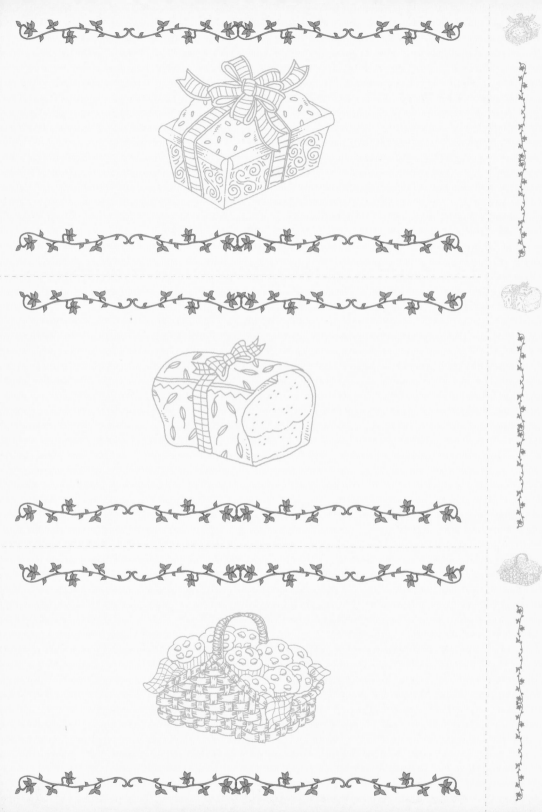

A gift from the kitchen of _____

For: _____

A gift from the kitchen of _____

For: _____

A gift from the kitchen of _____

For: _____

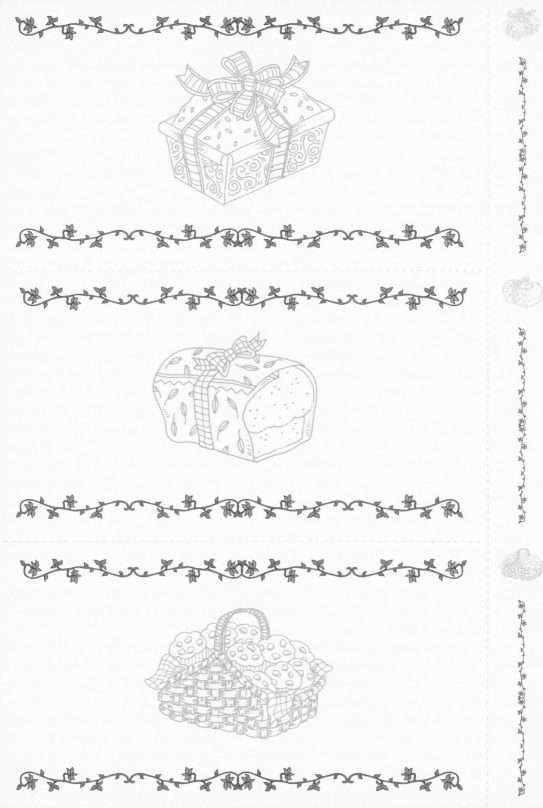

A gift from the kitchen of_____

For: _____

A gift from the kitchen of_____

For: _____

A gift from the kitchen of_____

For: _____

A gift from the kitchen of _____

For: _____

A gift from the kitchen of _____

For: _____

A gift from the kitchen of _____

For: _____